W9-AQD-787

McLEAN MERCER REGIONAL LIBRARY
BOX 505
RIVERDALE, ND 58565

The Checkered Flag

Motorcycle Racing

Billie B. Brooklyn

PowerKiDS press

New York

Published in 2015 by **The Rosen Publishing Group, Inc.**
29 East 21st Street, New York, NY 10010

Library of Congress Cataloging-in-Publication-Data

Brooklyn, Billie.
Motorcycle racing / by Billie Brooklyn.
p. cm. — (The checkered flag)
Includes index.
ISBN 978-1-4994-0167-7 (pbk.)
ISBN 978-1-4994-0140-0 (6-pack)
ISBN 978-1-4994-0158-5 (library binding)
1. Motorcycle racing — Juvenile literature. I. Brooklyn, Billie. II. Title.
GV1060.B76 2015
796.7—d23

Copyright © 2015 by The Rosen Publishing Group, Inc.

All rights reserved. No part of this book may be reproduced in any form
without permission in writing from the publisher, except by a reviewer.

Developed and produced for Rosen by BlueAppleWorks Inc.
Art Director: T. J. Choleva
Managing Editor for BlueAppleWorks: Melissa McClellan
Designer: Joshua Avramson
Photo Research: Jane Reid
Editor: Marcia Abramson

Photo Credits: cover David Acosta Allely/Shutterstock; title page Gines Romero/Shutterstock; TOC, p. 12 top
Walter Arce/Dreamstime; p. 4–5 bottom sainthorant daniel/Shutterstock; p. 5 left PhotoStock10/Shutterstock; p.
5 right top Chen WS/Shutterstock; p. 5 right bottom Christian Vinces/Shutterstock; p. 6–7 bottom National Photo
Company Collection/Library of Congress/Public Domain; p. 8 top Ahmad Faizal Yahya/Shutterstock; p. 8–9, 10
left, 11 right © Natursports/Dreamstime; p. 9 right Gines Romero/Shutterstock; p. 10–11 bottom Tomas Hajek/
Dreamstime; p. 11 left © Ahmad Faizal Yahya/Dreamstime; p. 12–13 bottom Kingarion/Shutterstock; p. 12 bottom
EvrenKalinbacak/Shutterstock; p. 13 right Elambeth/Creative Commons; p. 14 © Leon Switzer/Keystone Press;
p. 15 Agljones/Creative Commons; p. 16–17 bottom Autohausdolby/Public Domain; p. 16 top Silex/Creative
Commons; p. 16 bottom David Acosta Allely/Shutterstock; p. 17 right Lcodbar/Creative Commons; p. 18–19
bottom Ventura69/Dreamstime; p. 18 left, 19 right Igor Simanovskiy/Shutterstock; p. 20 Pukhov Konstantin/
Shutterstock; p. 20–21 bottom Fallenangel/Dreamstime; p. 21 right Warren Price/Dreamstime; p. 22–23 bottom
Diego Barbieri/Shutterstock; p. 22 left Anthony Aneese Totah Jr/Dreamstime; p. 24–25 Mark Fleming, GOGO Visual/
Creative Commons; p. 26–27 PhotoStock10/Shutterstock; p. 27 right Steindy/Creative Commons; p. 28 B.Stefanov/
Shutterstock

Manufactured in the United States of America
CPSIA Compliance Information: Batch #CW15PK: For Further Information contact: Rosen Publishing, New York, New York at 1-800-237-9932

Table of Contents

What Is Motorcycle Racing?   4

The First Motorcycle Races   6

On the Road   8

Grand Prix (MotoGP)   10

Superbike (WSBK) Racing   12

Isle of Man TT Racing   14

Endurance Road Racing   16

Off the Road   18

Motocross   20

Supercross   22

Enduro and Cross-Country   24

Track Racing   26

You and Motorcycle Racing   28

Glossary   30

For More Information   31

Index   32

What Is Motorcycle Racing?

Motorcycle racing is fast, exciting, and sometimes dangerous. There are on- and off-road race courses, **circuits**, open courses, and track races. The four main types of motorcycle race are:

- Road racing
- Motocross
- Enduro and cross-country
- Track racing

Men and women race against each other in all categories except motocross, which has separate events. Motocross racing is the best place for a kid to start. Riders as young as four years old can compete.

Motocross races are run over natural and human-made terrain courses with hills, jumps, and tight turns.

Road Racing

Road racing is held on paved, closed-course circuits across the country. Races can take place either on circuits built just for racing or on closed public roads. The latest generation of sportbikes are being stretched to the limit at road-racing events. Although the top classes run the courses at enormous speeds, there are also classes for riders on less-powerful machines.

Road racing is the racing of motorcycles on **tarmac**.

Enduro races run on harsh routes that include wooded and desert terrain.

In track racing, teams or individuals race opponents around an oval track.

The First Motorcycle Races

It's hard to tell exactly who invented the first motorcycle, since a few different inventors in Europe came up with the same idea at the same time. It all began with something called the "safety bicycle" which had two wheels of equal size and a pedal-crank mechanism on the rear wheel. In 1901, the Hendee Manufacturing Company came out with a 1.75-horsepower, single-cylinder motorcycle with the brand name of Indian. In 1903, the first Harley-Davidson was made. The rest is racing history.

In 1921, a Harley-Davidson ridden by Otto Walker was the first motorcycle ever to win a race at an average speed greater than 100 mph (160 km/h).

Dangerous Beginnings

Motordromes were wooden tracks built especially for motorcycle and car races. Their corners were steeply banked, making for a pretty wild ride. By the 1930s, board-track races were stopped because they were just too fast and too dangerous.

The original name for what we now know as motocross was a British off-road event called scrambles. The first-ever scramble was held in 1924 at Camberley, Surrey, in England. After a bit of a makeover from the French, including shorter tracks, added **laps,** and obstacles such as jumps, motocross was born. The name is a blend of the words "motorcycle" and "cross-country." Grafton, Vermont, hosted the first motocross race held in the United States in 1959.

⚠ FAST FACT

"Murderdrome" was the nickname for the motordrome tracks that endangered both riders and spectators of the races.

Board-track racing was popular in the United States during the 1910s and 1920s.

On the Road

On-road racing happens on a paved circuit or track or on closed public roads. Some of the best-known road races are the Grand Prix (MotoGP), Superbike (WSBK), AMA Pro Road Racing, and the World **Endurance** Isle of Man TT Race.

All racers wear helmets and protective suits.

All racers want to go fast so they can be first, but road bikes are designed to go superfast. Just imagine traveling at 350 mph (563 km/h) on a motorcycle!

How do they reach these speeds? A very skilled driver is obviously important, but the design of the bike and the engine power matter, too. Different road races have different engine power requirements.

To make turns at fast speeds, racers lean the bikes so far over that their knees sometimes touch the pavement.

ROAD-RACING BIKES

Bikes for road racing are typically narrow and weigh 300 pounds (136 kgs) or more. They have special smooth tires suited to gripping asphalt at high speeds and sharp angles. Their engine power is determined by the number of **engine strokes** and cubic centimeters (**ccs,** pronounced "see sees") of **displacement**, which is a measure of how much fuel is going through the engine. Bigger engines have more ccs, produce more power, and go faster.

Road-racing bikes are sleek and narrow, built for speed.

Grand Prix (MotoGP)

The Grand Prix is the Formula One of motorcycle racing, a premier world championship series of 18 races held in 14 countries on five different continents.

In the United States, the first Grand Prix motorcycle event was held at Daytona International Speedway in Florida in 1963. The race eventually was moved to California and held there until 2013. Now there are two races in the U.S. that are a part of the Grand Prix motorcycle racing season. One is the Indianapolis Grand Prix, which began in 2008. The other is the Grand Prix of the Americas, which was started in 2013 in Texas.

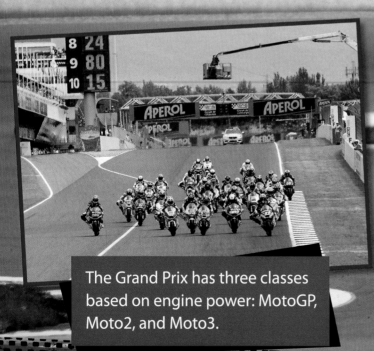

The Grand Prix has three classes based on engine power: MotoGP, Moto2, and Moto3.

Pros Only

Grand Prix-level road-racing bikes are specially built for professional racing only. They are not sold in everyday motorcycle shops, as it would be very dangerous for a nonprofessional to operate one. And even if you are trained, it isn't legal to drive one of these bikes on a regular road.

MARC MARQUEZ

Marc Marquez is the current world champion of MotoGP racing. Born in Spain in 1993, he got his first motorbike as a gift from his parents when he was just four years old. He later switched from Enduro to road racing and competed in the 2008 Portuguese Grand Prix at the age of 15. He was the youngest Spanish racer to earn a pole position or to win a top three finish in a world championship.

Marc Marquez celebrates at MotoGP Grand Prix of Catalunya in 2013.

Superbike (WSBK) Racing

Superbikes are modified motorcycles that are available to the public. Superbike races could be compared to touring car races. The official international championship series is called the Superbike World Championship. National championships are also held in many countries, including Australia, Canada, Japan, the United Kingdom, and the United States. The number one North American organization for this kind of racing is **AMA** Pro Racing.

At first, some people thought superbike racing was not as good as the motorcycle Grand Prix, but that has changed. The Superbike World Championship is now a world-class series featuring professional racers. Many riders who compete in WSBK have become famous among motorcycle racing fans.

Riders fight for best position during a race.

Kawasaki motorcycles are among the best known racing motorcycles.

Europe Rules!

The Superbike World Championship season is made up of a series of rounds. There are two races per round, and the results of these determine the competitors for the two annual world championships. The rounds are held at permanent tracks. Europe is the center of the action for Superbike racing but rounds have also been held in the United States and other places around the world.

Some of the best-known superbike manufacturers are Ducati, Honda, BMW, Suzuki, Kawasaki, MV Agusta, and Aprilia.

⚠ FAST FACT

The fastest superbike in the world may be the Dodge Tomahawk, a concept, or experimental, vehicle. Only nine people are known to own a Tomahawk, which cost $555,000 each and cannot be driven legally on regular roads. According to the manufacturer, it can achieve 0-60 mph (0-96.5 km/h) in 2.5 seconds and can reach a top speed of 400 mph (644 km/h).

In theory, the Dodge Tomahawk is the fastest bike on Earth. There has been no driver yet willing to prove the claim in practice.

Isle of Man TT Racing

One of the most famous motorcycle races is the International Isle of Man TT (Tourist Trophy) Race held on the Isle of Man, which is part of the United Kingdom. This Tourist Trophy race is so dangerous that they close the public roads it travels on the Isle of Man. Think potholes, telephone poles, and all kinds of obstacles popping up on the racer's path. The 37-mile (60 km) mountain course attracts riders from the United States, the United Kingdom, Belgium, Holland, and France, among other places.

The first race was held in 1907 and it's been going strong ever since.

Endurance Road Racing

Endurance racing tests the **durability** of motorbikes and the staying power of drivers. A team made up of multiple drivers tries to cover a great distance in a single event. In one type of race, drivers must cover as much distance as possible in lap form as fast as possible. Another type of race is about covering as much distance as possible in a set amount of time. A common endurance race length is 620 miles (1,000 km). Some races are much longer, covering 1,000 miles (1,609 km) and taking up to 24 hours to finish. That's endurance.

The Bol d'Or is a motorcycle endurance race held once a year in France. The **grueling** race lasts for 24 hours.

The Circuit des 24 Heures in France is a semipermanent racecourse most famous as the venue for the 24 Hours of Le Mans auto race.

Top Championship

The Federation of International Motorcycling (**FIM**) Endurance World Championship got started in 1960. It is the world's top endurance-racing championship. It is made up of a series of long-distance events. Until 2000, individual drivers with the most points won the championship. In 2001 they changed the rules and now the whole team of drivers is awarded the championship title.

All bikes in races such as the Suzuki 8 Hours in Japan, the 24 Hours of Le Mans Moto, and the Bol d'Or (Golden Bowl) must be **production-based**. That means the manufacturer offers a version of the same motorcycles for general purchase by the public.

Drivers run to their bikes at the beginning of an Enduro road race.

OFF-ROAD BIKES

An off-road motorcycle is much lighter than a road-racing bike and taller, too. Some bike seats are as high as 36 inches (91 centimeters). Made from aluminum instead of heavier metals, the sturdy suspension system is visible. The wheels aren't smooth like on-road tires. They're knobby so they can grip mud, rocks, sand, and gravel on the courses. Large plastic fenders at the front and back help reduce (but not eliminate) the amount of dirt spraying up at the driver.

Off-road bikes are light and sturdy with a great suspension system for jumping.

Motocross

Motocross races happen no matter what the weather is up to. Racers can count on a lot of mud if the rain lets loose on ungroomed dirt tracks. Riders suit up and face between a half to two miles (805 m to 3.2 km) of steep hills, twisty dirt roads, and muddy hairpin turns, as well as potholes and camelbacks, which are a series of humps in the road all in a row. Up to 40 riders can compete at once on a typical course. A professional motocross race offers two races or motos for each motorcycle class. Each moto is 30 noisy minutes long plus two full laps around the track. Points are earned according to where the rider finishes in each moto. The rider who scores the most points overall is declared the winner.

Children begin riding motocross as young as four years of age, riding 50cc bikes which are lighter and easier to control. The protective suit makes it hard to walk, so you might feel a bit like a robot when you try to walk in full motocross gear.

Many great motorcycle racers started their careers with motocross at a very young age.

AMA Series

The American Motorcyclist Association (AMA) holds the Motocross Championship Series every year starting in early May. There are 24 races on 12 tracks all across the United States. The races take place on Sundays. These great races are as much fun for spectators as they are for racers.

ASHLEY FIOLEK

Although she was born deaf, that didn't stop Ashley Fiolek from getting involved in one of the noisiest sports in the world. At age seven she jumped on her first 50cc and never looked back. She made her name in her rookie year of professional motocross by beating out the five-time Women's Motocross Association champ, Jessica Patterson. By doing so she became the youngest WMA champion of all time. In total, she's won the WMA Championship four times.

Ashley Fiolek, who was born in 1990, has retired from women's motocross racing but does not plan to stop riding moto.

Supercross

In the sport of supercross, off-road motorcycles race on a track filled with steep jumps and obstacles. The tracks are usually built inside professional sports stadiums, although one supercross race is held at Daytona International Speedway, a major auto racing venue. From January to May, supercross races take place on groomed tracks in major cities. Supercross is a very technical sport. The jumps and obstacles are even bigger than they are in motocross but the races are shorter. The first-ever supercross happened in 1972 at Los Angeles Coliseum.

Supercross races are very popular and usually get a lot of television coverage.

Championship Races

The AMA/FIM Supercross Series is an exciting series of motorcycle races held throughout North America. The two main classes that race at this level are Supercross (450cc bikes) and Supercross Lites (250cc bikes). Both classes ride bikes with four-stroke engines. The AMA awards three different championships: Supercross Champion, Supercross Lites East and Supercross Lites West Champions. Other organizations around the world offer a world championship title.

⚠ **FAST FACT**

Riders without factory sponsorship are called privateers. With limited sponsorship, they must often buy their own equipment and pay their own race fees and travel costs.

Supercross races are often held indoors in roof-covered stadiums.

Enduro and Cross-Country

Much like on-road endurance racing, Enduro focuses on the driver's ability to go the distance. Using modified motocross bikes (often with supersized gas tanks), riders tackle courses that take several hours or days to complete. The bikes may also need to have certain street-legal components if the race takes them onto public roads. Quieter exhaust systems and headlights are a couple of examples of the required add-ons.

A cross-country rally is a much longer race that uses bigger bikes than other off-road sports events. Drivers travel for several days, covering hundreds of miles on open off-road terrain. Cross-country races are popular with motorcycle drivers and fans all over the world. One of the most famous is the Dakar Rally. Other popular races include the Baja 1000 in Mexico, the Central Europe Rally in Hungary and Romania, the Baja Russia Northern Forest, the Trans Anatolia Rally Raid in Turkey, and the Rallye des Pharaons in Egypt.

THE DAKAR RALLY

The Dakar Rally is a famous race that used to travel from Paris to Dakar, the capital and largest city of Senegal, a country in West Africa. Since 2009 the race has taken place in South America. It's considered one of the toughest races in the world, taking around two weeks to complete. The Dakar, as it is called, crosses much tougher terrain than in other races. Drivers must cope with mountains, canyons, sand dunes, and desert. To do this, they use bikes that are built for off-roading, rather than modified on-road motorcycles. The race is divided into several stages of varying distances, some as long as 500–560 miles (800–900 km) per day.

Track Racing

Track racing takes place on an oval track where teams or individual racers ride to win by completing four to eight laps. Different kinds of races are held on different types of tracks, which are made of granite, shale, sand, grass, or even ice. The racers slide their bikes sideways on the surface, so that they power-slide or broadside into the bends. On the straight parts of the course, the bikes can go as fast as 68 mph (110 km/h).

Many races, both in the United States and abroad, use the speedway format on a dirt or shale track. In speedway racing, four riders race over four laps after a standing start. Points are awarded to all but the last-place finisher and are totaled up to determine a winner.

Ice racing is a wintry version of speedway racing. The motorcycles used have either all-rubber or studded tires, which determines their racing class. Riders lap counterclockwise around a track covered in a thick layer of ice. The studded tires require drivers to lean the bikes so far over on turns that their handlebars nearly touch the ice.

TRACK RACING BIKES

Customized motorcycles are used for track racing. These bikes have no brakes and only one gear. They use **methanol** for fuel, which gives them more speed and power. In speedway racing, the bikes have no gears and no rear suspension. It takes a lot of skill to control a motorcycle in track racing while going fast enough to win!

In ice racing, steel studded tires cut through ice and keep bikes from sliding.

You and Motorcycle Racing

Have you always wanted to try riding a motorcycle? Motocross is the most popular way for young riders to enter the exciting world of motorcycle racing.

It's probably a good idea to buy a used motocross bike at first to see if you really enjoy the sport. Protective head, eye, and body coverings are very important, because although this is a fun sport, it has some risks. Never ride a dirt bike without a helmet and proper protection for your hands, feet, and, well…all of you!

Riding motocross is about more than just riding laps, and the sooner you develop good form, the sooner you'll learn new tricks. Before you start, you will need to learn about the signal flags that are used to send messages to the drivers on the track. The flags warn about hazards and indicate the start and end of the race. When you feel ready, and after a few practice races with riders a little better than yourself, sign up for a real race and see how you do. Motocross is an amazing way to have fun and keep fit.

Motorcycle Racing Flags

Green Flag
The start of a race or all-clear track conditions.

White Flag with Red Cross
This means that ambulances, safety vehicles, or emergency workers are on the course. Racers exercise caution.

Red Flag
The race has been stopped. Racers reduce their speed and proceed with caution to the starting area.

Black Flag
There is a problem with your motorcycle or a disqualification. Racers reduce their speed and proceed around the course to the pit area.

Stationary Yellow Flag
There is a potentially hazardous situation on or near the track. Passing is allowed. Racers exercise caution.

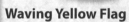

Waving Yellow Flag
There are serious hazards on or near the track. Racers proceed with caution.

Light Blue Flag with Diagonal Yellow Stripe
The racer is about to be overtaken by faster riders. The racer holds his or her line and does not interfere with their progress.

White Flag
The final lap of a race.

Checkered Flag
The end of a race or practice session. Racers move around the track or course to the designated exit.

Glossary

AMA The American Motorcyclist Association. The largest motorsports association in the world, it has 300,000 members. It oversees amateur and professional motorcycling events in the United States.

cc Cubic centimeter.

circuit A race track or course.

displacement The volume swept by all the pistons in the cylinders of an engine, an amount measured in cubic centimeters.

durability Ability to tolerate wear, pressure, and damage.

endurance The ability to keep going for long periods of time under challenging conditions.

engine stroke The backward and forward motions of a piston in a reciprocating engine are called strokes. There are motorcycles with two-stroke and four-stroke engines.

FIM The Fédération Internationale de Motocylisme (Federation of International Motorcycling) is the international governing body of 111 national motorcycling organizations.

grueling Very tiring, tough, and demanding conditions.

lap Completing a full circuit of the racetrack or course.

methanol A form of alcohol that can be used to fuel vehicle engines.

production-based motorcycle A motorcycle for racing that you can also buy versions of on the regular market.

tarmac A paving material made by covering layers of crushed rock with tar.

Index

McLEAN MERCER REGIONAL LIBRARY
BOX 505
RIVERDALE, ND 58565

A
American Motorcyclists Association (AMA) 8, 12, 21, 23
Aprilia 13

B
BMW 13
BMX 18
Bol D'Or 16, 17

C
circuit(s) 4, 5, 8, 15
cross-country rally 24

D
Dakar Rally 24, 25
Daytona International Speedway 10, 22
displacement 9
Ducati 13
durability 16

E
endurance race 16, 17, 24
Enduro 4, 5, 11, 17, 24

F
Federation of International Motorcycling (FIM) 17, 23
Fiolek, Ashley 21

G
goggles 18
Grand Prix 8, 10–12

H
Harley-Davidson 6
helmet 8, 18, 28
Hendee Manufacturing Company 6
Honda 13

I
Indianapolis Grand Prix 10
Isle of Man TT Race 8, 14, 15

K
Kawasaki 12, 13

L
lap 7, 15, 16, 20, 26, 28
Le Mans 24 Hours 17

M
Marquez, Marc 11
Miller, Mark 15
Motocross 4, 7, 20–22, 24, 28
MotoGP 8, 10, 11
Motordromes 7
MV Agusta 13

O
off-road racing 4, 7, 18, 22, 24, 25

R
road racing 4, 5, 8, 9, 11, 16, 23, 24

S
Speedway 10, 22,
speedway racing 26, 27
sportbikes 5
superbike 8, 12, 13, 15
supercross 22, 23
Suzuki 13, 17
Suzuki 8 Hours 17

T
track racing 4, 5, 7, 26, 27
TT Zero race 15